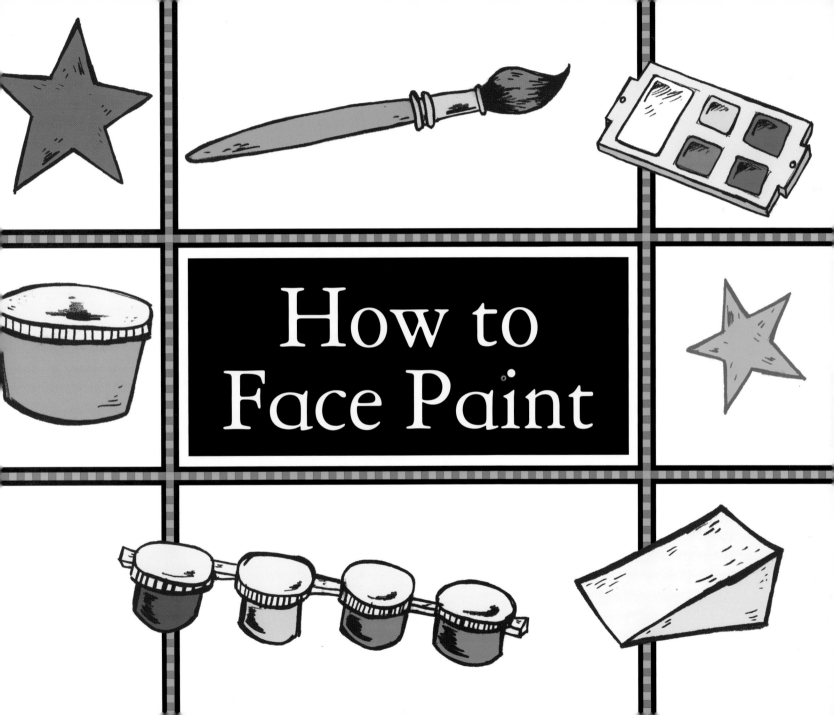

How to Face Paint

The Child's World

Published by The Child's World®
1980 Lookout Drive • Mankato, MN 56003-1705
800-599-READ • www.childsworld.com

Acknowledgments
The Child's World®: Mary Berendes, Publishing Director
Red Line Editorial: Editorial direction and production
The Design Lab: Design

Photographs ©: Mark Prytherch/Shutterstock Images, 4

ISBN: 978-1623235604
LCCN: 2013931351

Printed in the United States of America
Mankato, MN
July, 2013
PA02176

ABOUT THE AUTHOR

Megan Atwood lives in Saint Paul, Minnesota, with two cats. She face paints whenever she can.

ABOUT THE ILLUSTRATOR

Kelsey Oseid is an illustrator and graphic designer from Minneapolis, Minnesota. When she's not drawing, she likes to do craft projects, bake cookies, go on walks, and play with her two cats, Jamie and Fiona. You can find her work at www.kelseyoseid.com.

Table of Contents

Get Ready for Fun!

FESTIVAL FUN!
Does your town ever have **festivals** to celebrate holidays or other events? Sometimes you can get your face painted at these festivals. **Professional** face painters can turn you into almost anything. Ask your parents if any festivals are happening in your town!

Have you ever wanted to be a clown? Or a pirate? What about a puppy? It is easier than you think! Learn how to face paint. Then you can turn yourself and your friends into anything. Use your imagination!

This book will teach you how to paint different faces. Paint with a friend or a family member. Then you can paint each other's faces!

Make sure to get permission from your parents before face painting. You will need special supplies. Face painting can be messy. But it is also fun! Your parents can help you buy a face-painting kit. Kits have almost everything you need to start painting. You can also buy individual colors. Make sure you have the right tools before getting started.

You'll need:

- Face paint
- Old shirts to put over your clothes to keep them clean
- Covers for tables and chairs
- Washcloths and tissues
- Something to clean up messes—just in case!
- Brushes
- Sponges
- Soap and water
- Paper cups to put the water in

WHAT YOU'LL NEED:

- Black face paint
- Another color of face paint. Pick whatever color you want!
- Sponges and brushes
- Water for washing

Create a Superhero

You might not have superpowers. But painting a superhero face is super easy!

1 Start by dipping a brush in black face paint. Then draw the shape of an eye mask around your friend's eyes.

STEP 1

2 Next use whatever color you want to fill the mask in. You could make a supervillain by coloring the mask in black.

3 Let's give your superhero some style! You could give her dark eyebrows. Try adding patterns or new colors to the mask or her face.

Nice work on your superhero. Up, up, and away!

WHAT YOU'LL NEED:

- White face paint
- Pink face paint
- Black face paint
- Sponges and brushes
- Water for washing

Become a Bunny

It's time to hop around and wiggle your nose. With this project, you can help a friend turn into a bunny.

1 The first step is easy. Use a sponge and white face paint to color your friend's face. Almost his entire face should be white. Leave some space above his eyebrows.

STEP 1

STEP 2

2 Use the white sponge to draw bunny ears. Start right above one of the eyebrows. Then make an oval arc. The arc should go almost all the way to your friend's hairline. Now draw another one!

3 Next dip a clean sponge in the black face paint. Color the ears black. Then dip your sponge in the pink face paint. Color the tip of your friend's nose pink.

STEP 4

4 Take your black face paint and brush. Draw three dots under each of your friend's **nostrils**.

Now hop along to show off your new bunny!

WHAT YOU'LL NEED:

- Black face paint
- White face paint
- Red face paint
- Sponges and brushes
- Water for washing

Picture-Perfect Pirate

Ahoy, matey! Have you ever dreamed about looking for buried treasure? Get ready to turn a friend or family member into a pirate!

STEP 1

1 First have your friend close one eye. Very carefully color a black circle around her closed eye using the sponge.

STEP 2

2 Now dip a brush in black paint. Draw a line across your friend's forehead. The line should touch the top of the circle you drew.

3 Next use your brush to draw a mustache. You can also paint a pointy little beard on your friend's chin.

4 Now take your white face paint. Use a brush to draw polka dots above the black line you drew on your friend's forehead.

5 Now use the red face paint and sponge. Color all the space between the polka dots red. You've got a **bandana**!

You made a pirate. Let's hope she doesn't make you walk the plank!

WHAT YOU'LL NEED:
- White face paint
- Black face paint
- Face paint crayons
- Any other colors you want
- Sponges and brushes
- Water for washing

Clowning Around

Everyone loves a clown! There are lots of different ways you can give someone a clown face.

1 First comes the fun part. Use a sponge and white face paint to color your friend's face. His entire face should be white.

STEP
2

2 Then use a sponge to paint your friend's nose red. Use a red face paint crayon to make a big outline around his mouth. Use a sponge to color in the outline in red.

3 Next pick another color you like. Make an outline of a shape around each of your friend's eyes. Then color the shapes in. You could use a triangle. Or a diamond. Almost any shape will work!

4 Now put black face paint on a brush. Use the brush to outline all the shapes on your friend's face. Make sure to outline the red nose and red mouth, too!

Now you have a funny clown!

STEP 3

STEP 4

WHAT YOU'LL NEED:

- Black face paint
- White face paint
- Sponges and brushes
- Black face paint crayon
- Water for washing

Paint Your Own Puppy

Have you ever wanted a dog? Maybe you already have one! Follow the steps below to turn a friend into a friendly puppy.

STEP 1

1 First dip a brush in the black face paint. Use it to color the tip of your friend's nose black. Then draw a circle around your friend's eye. Color it in like you did in **Picture Perfect Pirate**.

2 Now take your black face paint crayon. Trace the outline of ears on either side of your friend's face. Start at the top of each eyebrow. The ears should go all the way down to his chin.

STEP
2

3 Next use your black face paint crayon. Outline your friend's mouth. Start from the edges of each nostril. End at each corner of his mouth. Draw a half moon shape under his bottom lip.

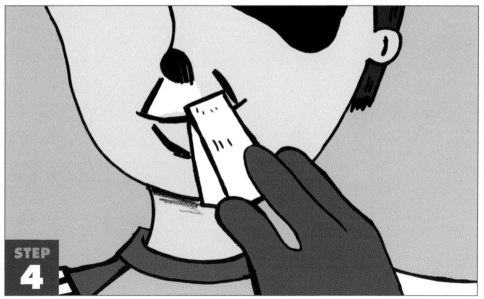

4 Now take another sponge. Dip it in the white face paint. Use the sponge to color in the ears and the mouth you drew.

STEP
5

CREATING A KITTY
Cats are another popular pet. Creating a kitty face isn't that different from painting a puppy face. Have an adult help you look for pictures of cats online or at your local library. How could you change your puppy face to look more like a kitty?

5 Finally use your black crayon to put three black dots under each nostril.

Now you have a puppy!

- Black face paint
- Your favorite face paint colors. You could use purple, pink, white, or even glitter!
- Brushes
- Black face paint crayon
- Water for washing

Be a Butterfly

Butterflies are beautiful **insects**. They are usually very colorful. Are you ready to paint a butterfly?

STEP 1

1 First dip a brush in the black face paint. Start at the inside of your friend's eye, near her nose. Draw a curved line that goes to the outer part of her eye. Then pull the line out and down to the middle of her cheek. Finish the line near her eye where you started. It should be shaped a little bit like a sideways heart.

2 Use the same black brush to draw a little butterfly body. The body can be shaped a bit like an **hourglass**. Start the body a little above your friend's eyebrow line. It should end in the middle of her nose.

3 Use the crayon to draw two lines on either side of the butterfly head. These lines are **antennas**. You can even put little dots at the ends.

STEP
3

STEP
4

TIME TO CLEAN UP
You have learned how to paint a puppy, a butterfly, a bunny, a pirate, a clown, and a superhero. Now it's time to clean up! Use a washcloth or tissue with soap and water to gently scrub off face paint. Wash out your brushes and sponges. Face painting can be messy! You'll need to clean the area where you were painting.

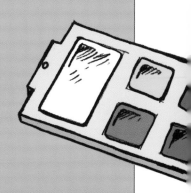

4 Now take your favorite colors and color in each side of the wings. Use colors and brushes to make fun designs. Use your imagination!

The best thing about painting a butterfly face is you can't go wrong! You can draw whatever you want. The sky's the limit!

Glossary

antennas (an-TEN-uhz): Antennas are feelers some animals use to sense their surroundings. Butterflies have a pair of antennas.

bandana (ban-DAN-uh): A bandana is a brightly colored square of cloth. A pirate often wears a bandana on her head.

festivals (FES-tuh-vuhlz): Festivals are celebrations that include fun activities. Many festivals have face painters.

hourglass (OUR-glas): An hourglass is an instrument people use to measure time. A butterfly's body can be shaped like an hourglass.

insects (IN-sektz): Insects are small animals without backbones that have wings. Butterflies are insects.

nostrils (NAH-struhlz): Nostrils are the two openings in a person's nose. Add three dots under each of your friend's nostrils when you are painting a puppy face.

professional (pruh-FESH-uh-nuhl): A professional is a person who does an activity for money instead of just for fun. A professional face painter can paint many kinds of faces.

Learn More

Books

Silver, Patricia. *Face Painting*. Toronto: Kids Can, 2000.

Watt, Fiona, Caro Childs, and Non Figg. *Starting Face Painting*.
London, UK: Usborne, 2005.

Web Sites

Visit our Web site for links about face painting: *childsworld.com/links*

Note to Parents, Teachers, and Librarians: We routinely verify our Web links to make sure they are safe and active sites. So encourage your readers to check them out!

Index